EXETER AIRPORT
In Peace and War

A PICTORIAL HISTORY

Geoff Worrall

DEVON BOOKS

Published in association with Exeter Airport

First published in Great Britain in 1988 by Devon Books

ISBN: 0 86114 835-5

British Library Cataloguing-in-Publication Data

Worrall, Geoff
    Exeter Airport 1938–1988: a pictorial history.
    1. Devon. Exeter. Airports. Exeter airport to 1988
    I. Title
    387.7'36'0942356

Printed and bound in Great Britain by Penwell Ltd, Callington, Cornwall for A. Wheaton & Co. Ltd, Exeter.

DEVON BOOKS
Official Publisher to Devon County Council

An imprint of Wheaton Publishers Ltd. A Member of Maxwell Pergamon Publishing Corporation plc

Wheaton Publishers Ltd
Hennock Road, Marsh Barton, Exeter, Devon EX2 8RP
Tel: 0392 74121; Telex 42794 (WHEATN G)

SALES
Direct sales enquiries to Devon Books at the address above.

Trade sales to: Town & Country Books, P.O. Box 31, Newton Abbot, Devon TQ12 5XH. Tel: 080 47 2541

CONTENTS

ACKNOWLEDGMENTS

GRATEFUL THANKS ARE extended to all who have helped to compile this Golden Jubilee history of Exeter Airport, including airport staff past and present, and in particular the former airport managers Harry Ellis and Wing Commander Jack Pearse.

The Airport would also like to thank the following for their assistance and co-operation.

The Editor of the *Express & Echo*, Mr John Budworth; *Echo* photographers past and present, and photographic processor Keith Hazell.

Exeter Flying Club Chief Flying Instructor, Wing Commander Ted King; pre-war Aero Club member Gordon Taylor; Sammy Samuel (CAACU); Joe Wasnoiwski (317 Polish Fighter Squadron); Mrs Mary Carnall of Clyst Honiton; Claude ('Ginger') Davies; Harry Richards (Air Traffic Control); Roy Smallridge (Communications); Colin Pugh (Airport welder) and aero enthusiasts Michael Payne and John Gregory.

The publishers thank the following individuals and organisations who kindly provided photographs for use in this book: *Express & Echo*, Exeter; Exeter Airport Archives; Noel Deeble; Joe Wasniowski; Ted King; John Gregory; Les Ginger; Harry Richards; Pete Morgan; George Pridmore; and to many others who have helped provide information and pictures.

Special thanks to Keith Fordyce, Director of the Torbay Aircraft Museum, who kindly provided material for use in the cover photograph. The photograph was taken by Peter Cooper.

INTRODUCTION

THE MAYOR OF EXETER said, on Exeter Airport's opening day, that 'the aim of the airport is utility, pleasure, convenience and commerce, but the Council recognises that it would be a valuable addition to the State in the defence of the country in an emergency'.

That emergency was soon to come, and the airport was indeed a valuable addition to the State during it. But the Mayor was speaking, on that July day in 1938, when war was on the horizon. In July 1988, not only has there been peace in Europe for forty-two years, but the future of that peace has never looked safer.

In the years since the war the airport has grown and developed, towards the aims of utility, pleasure, convenience and commerce. Growth in prosperity and technology have made leisure air travel available to all, and millions go by air each year on their holidays. Business air travel is growing as commerce between countries increases, and as speed becomes increasingly important.

This history tells some of the story, and especially it tells of the people who make it happen. We owe a debt to them all, but especially to my predecessors, Wing Commander, 'Parky' Parkhouse, Wing Commander Jack Pearse, and Mr Harry Ellis.

In 1988, the airport is crossing new thresholds. The Airports Act of 1986 led in 1987 to the creation of Exeter and Devon Airport Limited, by Devon County Council, to own and run the Airport. The removal of travel and trade barriers, together with deregulation of European air transport, will create new markets and give airlines and airports the means of serving them. Relocation of industry and increases in population in Devon and the South West mean a growing demand for business and leisure travel. Use of regional airports such as Exeter will increase as the major U.K. airports, and the airspace above them, reach saturation.

So, while in 1938 the prospects were for war in Europe, in 1988 we see prosperity and growth, although we remain mindful that we must defend that. Instead of looking at Europe on the brink of war, we are looking at Europe on the brink of real unity. Exeter Airport will, in the next fifty years, provide the air links to Europe and the rest of the world, for people and industry in Devon and the South West to use for leisure and business.

After fifty years of service, the airport's aims remain 'utility, pleasure, convenience and commerce.'

Jon Cousens
AIRPORT DIRECTOR

1

TAKE-OFF '38

FROM TINY PISTON-engined Hornet Moth biplane to sleek supersonic Concorde jet – that's the romantic story of the development of Exeter Airport spanning fifty years. Hornet Moths were part of the scene when the airport was officially opened on 30 July 1938 by the Secretary of State for Air, Sir Kingsley Wood. Concorde arrived almost half a century later, symbolizing for watching enthusiasts the dramatic advances those fifty years had brought both to the airport and the aircraft it handles.

The Hornet Moths landed on grass with a maximum run of 850 metres. For Concorde there was a reinforced permanent main runway of over 2000 metres, plus the very latest in instrument landing and radar surveillance systems.

In the years between those first Hornet Moths and Concorde, Exeter Airport has given a remarkable half century of service to the public in peace and war. The airport when Sir Kingsley Wood opened it in 1938 was a ninety acre grass-covered flying field on which first a hangar and then an impressive terminal building, mostly single storey, had been built. Flying had, though, been in progress for more than a year from a kind of 'tented terminal' which opened on 31 May 1937. Before the permanent buildings were completed, the fliers and the passengers used makeshift shelters, including from time to time marquees and tents. Mr Gordon Taylor, a member of the aero club of those days, remembers that the club had temporary quarters, including a bar at the back of the hangar, before it moved to more elegant quarters when the terminal building was ready.

The airfield had been carved from the land of Waterslade Farm, and in 1938 the farmhouse and farm buildings were still standing on the far boundary from the terminal, where today's main runway now crosses.

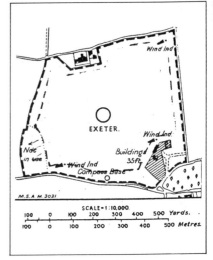

Exeter airport – plan and location map taken from Air Pilot magazine in 1939.

Information sheets supplied to visiting pilots stated that the surface conditions were grass covered, the field was 100 feet (31 metres) above mean sea level, and an obstruction requiring special caution was trees, fifty-five feet high on the south-east side. Special signals and lighting were non-existent. But facilities for aircraft included refuelling – aviation fuel, oil and fresh water. All normal repairs could be carried out and ground engineers were in attendance.

The field boasted one hangar, 90 feet wide, 65 feet deep and with a door height of 14 feet and width of 70 feet. Landing or taking off towards the south-west provided the longest run of 870 yards. Pilots were advised to use that

31 May 1937: The first airliner to land at Exeter, a Jersey Airways DH86, with W.B. Caldwell as pilot.

direction in conditions of no wind. From north to south the field measured 700 yards, from east to west 750, and from south-east to north-west, 780.

A large crowd turned up on 31 May 1937 when the 'tented terminal' officially opened to traffic. The two principal airlines then in operation were Jersey Airways, and Railway Air Services, using eight-to-ten-seater De Havilland Dragon Rapides.

The first airliner to use the airport was a Jersey Airways DH 86 flown by W.B. Caldwell. It arrived at 10.30 a.m. to a welcome by the Mayor of Exeter, Mr Alfred Anstey and council members. There too was twenty-five year old New York born Whitney Straight, son of Mrs L.K. Elmirst of Dartington Hall, Totnes, Devon, and founder and governing director of the Straight Corporation, which was to operate the airport on behalf of the council.

With Mr Straight were Anthony Chitty and Robert Hening, architects of the terminal building then under construction. They specially designed the building for eventual expansion as needed.

E.J. Mansfield, Chairman of the Estates Committee of the city council said it was unusual for a newly-opened aerodrome to have two regular air services. Mr Straight said he was delighted to be associated with an enterprise with such a fine future. With the available adjacent land, Exeter was as big as Croydon, if not bigger.

To mark the occasion the Jersey Airways DH 86 took the Mayor and other civic leaders for flips over the city centre. Two Short Scions from Plymouth flew in to join the celebrations, though the official opening ceremony was still to come just over a year later.

Ever since that first Jersey Airways machine arrived in May 1937, Channel Island lines have been associated with Exeter, apart from the disruption of the war years. Jersey European Airways remains Exeter's principal scheduled airline customer and has, since 1985, made the airport its operating, engineering and administrative headquarters.

The second passenger airline to arrive on that opening day of 1937 was a Railway Air Services flight, believed also to have been a Rapide. On board were officials of Railway Air Services and of the Great Western Railway.

The treasured 'Pleasure Flight' ticket from 1937. The day after the flight the pilot, Jack Mouatt, was badly hurt when the aircraft 'spun in' accidently.

The first commercial flight into Exeter was made by this Leopard Moth flown by Capt S.W. Scott, Chief Pilot of Air Despatch. He had flown from Hatfield on Coronation Day, 1937 rushing photographs of the Coronation of King George VI for the *Express & Echo*. Pictures were also flown to Plymouth and Penzance. One flight landed at Haldon with film of the Coronation for showing at Teignmouth's Riviera Cinema. Greeting Capt Scott is Mr W.R. Parkhouse of Haldon whose staff went to Exeter to handle the delivery flight.

Closely concerned with Westcountry aviation in the early days was Wing Commander Jack Pearse who now lives at Topsham, near Exeter. He remembers that the airport manager in 1937 was Captain L.R. ('Jock') Mouatt, a good pilot who had to give up flying after a most unfortunate accident when a Tiger Moth 'spun in' as he was instructing a pupil. It was said at the time that the pupil's foot caught under the rudder bar, and the plane spun down before he could disentangle it. Jock was so badly hurt he had to give up his job.

At the time of the accident, Jack Pearse who was on his way to Plymouth Airport to take up a post of manager. He was diverted by his employers, the Straight Corporation, who were operating Exeter Airport as well as Plymouth, to take over temporarily from Jock.

Mary Carnall of Clyst Honiton village remembers that on the day before the crash Captain Mouatt was taking passengers up on pleasure trips. One of them was Mrs Carnall's mother. The ticket cost five shillings (25p) and was kept by the family for many years until they gave it recently to the Airport's archives.

Wing Commander Pearse recalls that the early passenger services, using Rapides and later Airspeed Couriers, linked Exeter with Bristol, Jersey, the Scillies, Cardiff, Weston-super-Mare, Swansea and Plymouth. There were also charter flights to the Continent. Western Airways as well as Jersey Airways and Railway Air Services used Exeter. The Air Ministry were then paying a subsidy of sixpence per seat per mile to encourage people to start small airlines, and there were very high standards.

Exeter's football club began using the airport to attend away fixtures. One example was a Western Airways charter in the Autumn of 1938 for City's match with Cardiff.

Before this period, S.W. Scott made history as the pilot of the first commercial flight into Exeter. That was with a Leopard Moth in 1937 when he flew from London with pictures of the Coronation of King George VI for the *Express & Echo* newspaper.

When it was announced in 1938 that a civil air guard would be formed at the airport, more than three hundred local men and women were among the applicants, and a successful organisation was formed with C.R. Whytt appointed as organiser. Ansons of 217 Squadron RAF flew in to give the members air experience, and one of the chief flying instructors around that time was Flying Officer T.K. Breakell.

Aero club activities between 1937 and 1939 played a major part in the life of the airport. Roughly half of the space in the new terminal building was allocated to the club which had its own spacious dining room, lounge with bar, changing rooms and squash courts. The courts have since been absorbed into today's conference room suite. Miles Magisters, Hillson JAP ultra-light trainers, Hornet Moths and Tiger Moths were used for flying tuition.

At the outbreak of war, the aerodrome itself was requisitioned by the Air Ministry, and as it was transformed into an RAF station, local lanes leading to the airfield were cordoned off and entry restricted by guards.

Imperial Airways, Railway Air Services and British Airways flew a number of their civil aircraft to Exeter to be dispersed to the perimeter of the airfield awaiting use in National Air Communications by the government.

SOFT LANDINGS

AVIATION TYCOON WHITNEY Straight took a personal interest in seeing the airfields he built in the 1930s were good ones.

Seventy-nine year old Reg Lobb of Barley Mount, Exeter, who was a lorry driver engaged in the construction of Exeter Airport between 1936 and 1938, recalls: 'Early in the job I was working for Eastmond's of Exeter when I was ordered to take a six-wheeler lorry out to the site of the airfield. It had to be loaded to make a total weight with the lorry of ten tons.

'When I got there this American gentleman Whitney Straight got into the passenger seat and told me to drive the lorry over various parts of the field. As I did so, he made a diagram showing all the soft places where the lorry sank in, so that he would know where attention needed to be given for aircraft to land.'

Reg later delivered loads of bricks for the construction of the airport's first terminal building. He and his wife Louise were invited along to join other guests for the grand opening and air display on 30 July 1938.

2

ON SITE

WHEN YOU WANT to build an airport, how do you find the best place to put it? That was the question confronting officers and members of Exeter City Council as they scanned the surrounding countryside in 1930.

They called in a leading expert of that time to help them find the answer, a real-life 'Biggles' of the First World War. He flew over the Exeter area making the aerial survey needed to locate the best airport site. He was Commander William Francis Forbes-Sempill, the Master of Sempill and heir to Lord Sempill.

During the 1914–18 War he had a distinguished flying career in the Royal Flying Corps and the Royal Naval Air Service, being awarded the Air Force Cross. He became a notable member of the Royal Aeronautical Society and in the years from 1924 to 1930 was a competitor in the King's Cup round-Britain air race.

The Commander, who by the time Exeter Airport was officially opened in July, 1938 had become the 19th Baron Sempill, headed the survey which guided the city council of the 1930s to its choice of farmland at Clyst Honiton, some six miles from the city centre, as the site for the city's airport.

Time has shown how wise his advice was. The site is nearly always fog free, has an enviable record for weather, and with the River Exe estuary as an unmistakable landmark, is comparatively easy to find when there is poor visibility – a fact raiding Luftwaffe pilots took advantage of during the Second World War.

In 1936 the city council acquired the small dairy holding Waterslade Farm from the Church Commissioners. Then began the building of the airport, on a much smaller area of land than today's airport occupies. The original purchase was 186 acres.

Contractors levelled 90 acres to make the airfield, leaving the remainder for future expansion. A terminal building, still in use today as part of the much larger terminal, was designed. The architects were Robert Hening and A.M. Chitty and the main contractors the Exeter builders Soper and Ayers. Involved as City Surveyor was Robert Dymond. The Town Clerk at that time was Cyril Newman.

Like many other developing civil airports of its day, Exeter relied on grass runways. It wasn't until the Air Ministry requisitioned the site for the Royal Air Force at the outbreak of the Second World War that the field was expanded and

The men who played a leading role in the development of Exeter airport appear in this historic photograph. Wing Commander W.R. 'Parky' Parkhouse (fourth from left), and Whitney Straight (sixth from left) whose Straight Corporation formed Exeter Airport Ltd.

The occasion was the retirement of Parkhouse as Airport Manager in 1956. His successor as manager, Wing Commander Jack Pearse is on the extreme right. Whitney Straight flew down for the farewell party in a BOAC De Havilland Devon.

Also pictured L to R are: Airport Secretary S.J. Cox; Chairman, Roland King-Farlow; Engineering Director, Freddie Jeans; Mr Parkhouse's wife, Vera; and Chief Accountant, T.F. Allen.

three solid runways built on conventional RAF 'directional' lines. The ministry acquired parts of Fairoak Farm and Ware's Farm, also from the Church Commissioners, to make the aerodrome three times its original size.

More land was bought in 1955 for further extensions and in 1959 the Ministry of Defence bought the original site of the airport from Exeter City Council.

No longer needing the airfield by April 1972, the Ministry sold it to a consortium of the Devon County Council, Exeter City Council and Torbay Borough Council, and in April 1974, on local government reorganisation, Devon County Council took over.

In 1987 ownership of the airport was taken over by a limited company, Exeter and Devon Airport Ltd, in accordance with a directive from the Secretary of State for Transport under the Airports Act, 1986. The shareholding in the company is 100 per cent owned by the County Council, and the policy of inviting a private company to look after the commercial operation of the airport was continued; a policy originally introduced by the old Exeter City Council in 1937. From the early days the names of two men loom large, William 'Parky' Parkhouse and Whitney Straight.

Wing Commander Parkhouse, a Royal Navy Air Service Pilot in the 1914–18 war, was boss of Agra Engineering based in Teignmouth, Devon. He was the man who opened the airfield at Haldon in 1929, high on the heathland above Teignmouth. It was Devon's first airport, used both by private fliers and passenger services, notably Railway Air Services. The Wing Commander was eventually to become one of the most distinguished managers of Exeter airport.

While still at Haldon, Parkhouse was approached by a young man of sixteen asking for flying lessons. Whitney Straight was on his way up in the aviation business and it was 'Parky' Parkhouse of Haldon who taught him to fly while he was still a Cambridge student.

Whitney Straight obtained his pilot's licence aged seventeen. He was the son of Mrs L.K. Elmhirst of Dartington Hall, Totnes, and he later became a key figure in the formation of Exeter Aero Club before the Second World War. It was his company, Exeter Airport Ltd, part of the Straight Corporation, which in the late 1930's became the first official operator of Exeter Airport for the city council.

Another keen young flier involved in those early days of Exeter Airport was Jack Pearse, mentioned in the previous chapter. Like Parkhouse, he was to become a long-serving manager of the airport. Formerly a clerk in a Plymouth insurance office, his flying days began after he won a pilot training course in a competition organized by Lord Beaverbrook's *Daily Express*. As a result he became a Straight Corporation pilot.

Pearse recalls an early flight: 'I landed at Exeter in 1937, before it became an aerodrome, to see what it was like, on behalf of Whitney Straight, who was keen to see an airfield developed there.'

Jack Pearse became temporary manager of the airfield in 1937, after the unfortunate accident which ended the flying days of his predecessor, Captain L.R. 'Jock' Mouatt. He stayed until 1938 when he was succeeded by Flt Lt R.L. Bateman who was manager at the time of the official opening ceremony by Kingsley Wood.

But Bateman himself had only a short reign, and when he left in 1939 Haldon's Bill Parkhouse took over, remaining until all civil flying ended when Exeter was requisitioned by the Air Ministry at the start of the Second World War.

Parky went off to be an Engineering Officer in the RAF and Jack Pearse to be a Flying Officer. Both were to reach the rank of Wing Commander in outstanding wartime careers. After the war Parky returned to Exeter in 1947 where he remained as manager until his retirement in 1956, when he was succeeded by Jack Pearse.

One of his innovations at the Airport – he was keenly interested in Devon agriculture – was a grass drying plant which converted grass cut from the airfield into cattle fodder.

Parkhouse was also involved in reopening the Aero Club in 1949.

In the years between 1945 and the airport's Golden Jubilee in 1988, the Airport has had only four managers – Parky, Jack Pearse and Harry Ellis who were all employed by Exeter Airport Ltd., and the present Airport Director, Jon Cousens of Airports UK, who succeeded Exeter Airport Ltd as operators for Devon County Council in 1984.

The terminal buildings and hangar viewed across the airfield prior to the official opening in 1938. The 'path' in the foreground was part of a marker circle in the centre of the field.

Exeter Airport Ltd was part of the Straight Corporation from its inception up to 1959, when Harper Aviation took over. Harper's sold out in 1964 to Air Holdings, parent company of Airwork, and through Exeter Airport Ltd, they operated the terminal until Airports UK took over in 1984.

A FLAT HILL

AN IRISH STATESMAN on a visit to Exeter Airport was quick to spot the reason for its success as an airfield.

Accorded the VIP treatment by the then manager Wing Commander Jack Pearse in 1959, the Irish Foreign Minister observed: 'What a nice flat hill you have here!'

A touch of the blarney perhaps, but he'd seen that the airfield's plateau location made it the ideal site for an airport.

With the Irish President, the minister had returned by sea from the USA to Plymouth, and they had travelled to Exeter to catch a flight to Dublin.

Wing Commander Pearse, incidentally, worked for the jet engine pioneer Sir Frank Whittle in his Power Jets organisation immediately after the Second World War, but he says: 'I wanted to get back into flying so I bullied Whitney Straight into starting up his aerodromes again, and in 1947 I re-opened Plymouth for the Straight Corporation.'

One of the late Wing Commander Parkhouse's three sons, John Parkhouse, is now Group Managing Director with British Aerospace at Stevenage.

3

OPENING DAY

WHEN HE OFFICIALLY opened Exeter Airport on 30 July 1938, the then Secretary of State for Air, the Rt. Hon. Sir Kingsley Wood MP described it as: 'A very sound investment for the future.'

His words were to prove true in the world war that was soon to follow, and in the many years of peace since. The airfield played a vital role both in attack and defence during the war, and fifty years later is achieving new records for peacetime traffic.

The investment Sir Kingsley spoke about in fact amounted to £35000 in cash terms. That's what the airport originally cost Exeter City Council.

Meeting in the city's thirteenth-century Guildhall, the councillors agreed that Exeter must have an airport. Some though considered the £35000 cost was too much for the city's ratepayers to fork out. They submitted that since the airfield

Sir Kingsley Wood speaking at the opening ceremony, 30 July 1938. Seated L to R: Whitney Straight; Sir Francis Shelmerdine, Director General of Civil Aviation; J.G.R. Orchard, Sheriff of Exeter.

would undoubtedly be a great defence asset in time of war, the government should subsidise it. The councillors nevertheless voted by a narrow majority of two in favour of going ahead, with the ratepayers footing the bill.

On that grand opening day the weather conditions were out of character for the airfield, and low cloud meant that the spectacular air display arranged for the occasion had to be restricted, though it did go ahead.

An estimated 30000 people turned up for the event, and more than a thousand cars and motorcycles were parked on the airfield site without difficulty. Sir Kingsley arrived in an aircraft of 24 Communications Squadron of the RAF, a De Havilland 86. The flight from Croydon had taken an hour and a quarter 'against a strong head wind'.

An *Express & Echo* report described the new airport as one of a chain operated by the Straight Corporation Ltd of which the governing director was Whitney Straight, 'a practical visionary whose faith in the future of aviation was as marked as his tireless energy and gift for organisation'.

Whitney Straight flew down in his own light aircraft to join the Mayor of Exeter, Mr R.J. Rew, and Sheriff, Mr Jack Orchard (proprietor of the Royal Clarence Hotel), in welcoming the Secretary of State for Air.

Mr Straight, then twenty-five years old, was Chairman of the flourishing Exeter Aero Club which was quartered in the new terminal building. Jack Orchard was the club's vice chairman, and the Lord Lieutenant of Devon, Earl Fortescue, who was among the guests for the opening, was the club's President.

The *Express & Echo* reported that Exeter had joined the ranks of important centres in Great Britain which were equipped with modern airports. The new terminal buildings would enable Exeter to keep abreast of developments in the age of air travel, thus maintaining the importance it had attained as a centre for road and rail traffic.

Joining the civic leaders in welcoming VIP guests was the airport manager Flt Lt R.L. Bateman. The guests included the Lord Mayor of Cardiff, and the Mayor of Weston-super-Mare, and representatives of the foreign air attaches in London. Passenger air links had already been formed between Exeter, Weston-super-Mare and Cardiff.

The Mayor told the assembled company: 'The aim of the airport is utility, pleasure, convenience and commerce, but the council recognises that it would be a valuable addition to the State in the defence of the country in an emergency.' The report didn't comment on the response of three crack German aerobatic aces who were there for the air display!

The pilots were Herr Herwarth Wendel, a forty-one year old lawyer who had flown with the German Air Force in the First World War; Dr Karl Scherzer and Herr Emil Kropf, recent winner of the German aerobatic championship.

Herr Wendel's display was his first since recovering from a crash in which he had broken his neck. He thrilled the Exeter audience by traversing his 160hp Bucker Jungmeister machine upside down across the airfield. Applauded by the audience afterwards, he gave the Nazi salute in acknowledgement.

Dr Scherzer and Herr Kropf used an old open Klemm machine and a Focke Wulf Stieglitz biplane.

In the light of history one wonders if any of the three affable German aces ever returned to fly up the River Exe estuary during the Second World War with less friendly intentions!

At the opening ceremony E.J. Mansfield revealed that the search for a suitable site for a city airport began in 1930, and he praised Lord Sempill for having led the survey which decided on Clyst Honiton.

In declaring the airport open, Sir Kingsley, sporting a scarlet carnation in his buttonhole, declared: 'Exeter was the first city in the British Isles to cut a canal to allow seagoing vessels to reach an inland port. It has lost none of its spirit of enterprise, and now four hundred years after, it is in the forefront of municipalities in making provision for the newest form of transport.'

Recognising the importance of the Clyst Honiton site, the Air Ministry intended to establish meteorological and wireless stations there. Services were already operating through Exeter to Jersey, the Isles of Scilly, Bristol, Cardiff and the North of England.

Sir Kingsley praised the flourishing Exeter Aero Club and said he was delighted it had agreed to take part in the new Civil Air Guard scheme.

As Sir Kingsley spoke, a Saro 1840 hp 'London' flyingboat from Mount Batten, Plymouth roared overhead. Accompanying Sir Kingsley at the ceremony was the Director General of Civil Aviation, Sir Francis Shelmerdine.

The terminal building main entrance, 1938.

Welcoming the plan for met. and radio stations at Exeter, Whitney Straight said it meant aircraft could fly in and out with regularity and safety. Of the Civil Air Guard Scheme he said it would enable people aged eighteen to fifty, men and women, to become proficient pilots for as little as thirty shillings.

After the opening ceremony the Blue Ensign was flown from the mast of the terminal building.

A local 'ace' in the subsequent air display was Capt F.S. Symondson of Colyton who put his De Havilland Moth through a spectacular series of First World War aerobatics, and a 'falling leaf' demonstration. A glider demonstration by Dr Jack Dewsbery ran into trouble when the Cadet aircraft with which Capt G.W. Ferguson was towing him got into low cloud during which towing tension couldn't be maintained. The tow parted, and with yards of loose cable around the nose of his Rhonsperber glider's nose the doctor managed to put it down in a field bordering the airport, without damage.

The programme also included a fly-past and demonstration of Exeter Airport and Aero Club aircraft, along with an air drill by six Vickers Vildebeests of No 22 (Torpedo Bomber) Squadron, RAF.

Other aircraft in flight were a Westland Lysander Army Co-operation monoplane, and a Wicko plane piloted by G.N. Wikner of Southampton.

The *piece de resistance* was some polished formation flying by three Gloster

Sheriff of Exeter

Cnclr Cecil BROWN E. (Cmmttee).

J.G.R. ORCHARD. (Vice-Chairman Exeter Aero Club).

R.L. BATEMAN. (Manager).

F.S. LEE (Cmmttee).

W.R. PARKHOUSE.

WHITNEY STRAIGHT. (Chairman).

R.A. MILBURN. (Assnt Pilot).

K. KEY. (Fits in everywhere).

K.J. LANNAWAY. (Steward).

J. WILLS.

"Bob" DYMOND. (City Surveyor).

C.H. GRANT (Chief Ground Engineer).

M.E. CANN. (Administrator).

Capt Ronald BOLTON & Autogiro.

MISS FOLLETT.

Gordon TAYLOR.

Joe HIBBERD.

Exeter Airport Personalities of 1938 by Exeter artist George 'Stil' Stilling. George was a regular visitor to the Aero Club, and though not a pilot himself, often flew with friends.

Gauntlets of 151 Fighter Squadron RAF. Worsening weather meant they had to cut out a planned aerobatic display.

Grand finalé was a parachute descent by Mr Benno de Greeuw who made a neat landing on the airfield.

Local organisation was by the Airport Manager, Flt Lt Bateman, and the control officer was Bill Parkhouse from Haldon, destined himself to become the airport's first post-war manager.

4

WAR

FORTY YEARS AFTER the ending of the Second World War, an attractive woman in her sixties stood alone on an industrial site a stone's throw from the airport entrance, with tears running down her cheeks. They were tears of pride for the memory of her Hurricane pilot husband who was killed while flying from Exeter with his squadron during the war. She was just one of the thousands of men and women associated with the airfield during the war who now make nostalgic return visits to remember those grim yet glorious days.

When the mystery woman stopped at the car park kiosk near the airport entrance to ask attendant Claude ('Ginger') Davies if he could tell her where the wartime water tower was, she couldn't have asked a better person. Claude, 67, of Whipton, Exeter, is an airport veteran whose memories go right back to the war. A Bere Alston, Devon, man he was posted to Exeter in 1941 with 504 Nottingham Auxiliary Squadron of Hurricane fighters, as an airframe fitter.

Of that encounter with the woman inquirer he recalls: 'I was able to tell her that the water tower which served the massive wartime complex of living quarters on the other side of the Rockbeare Road from the terminal, wasn't there any more, but I took her as near as I could to the place where it was, where several of the original RAF buildings remain.

'She was remembering the site as I did, packed with living quarters, messes, a NAAFI canteen, stores, medical centre and a mortuary. I used to see the bodies of shot down German pilots taken to the mortuary.

'The woman told me that she served at Exeter in the Women's Auxiliary Air Force as a dental assistant, and her husband was a Hurricane pilot who was killed on a mission.

'When I showed her the site of the quarters she asked if I would leave her alone there so she could quietly try to remember the old days.

'A little later a man came to see me who turned out to be her second husband She had been posted to Pembroke from Exeter, and met her second husband who was a Sunderland pilot there.

'He told me: "She's standing over there all alone and in tears trying to visualise it as it was. But don't worry, she's delighted to have found again the place that holds so many memories for her".'

Ginger's crews lived in wooden huts beside the wartime airfield before the more permanent quarters were built. When the huts were damaged in one of

Claude 'Ginger' Davies.

Pilots of 504 (County of Nottingham) Squadron with one of their Hurricane fighters at Exeter during the War. One of them was Flying Officer (later Squadron Leader) Blair White whose widow Teresa today lives at Exmouth. He is the third from the left in the middle row. Teresa remembers that she and her husband stayed with a family in Hill Barton Road who gave them a very friendly welcome. The family's own RAF pilot son had been killed in action. Flying Officer White was shot down and wounded while defending Exeter in an enemy raid on the city in 1941. He was pursuing an enemy bomber. He later commanded two fighter squadrons in Malta until reported missing in July 1943. He is among the war heroes whose names are given on a memorial in Malta. The photograph has been loaned by his widow.

many German raids, the men were moved to a house in Pinhoe, but when on duty slept in bunks inside the surface shelters which formed part of the 'W' shaped aircraft pens around the airfield perimeter.

The lane from the A30 to the airfield entrance was closed and only officially approved traffic was allowed through. Ginger remembers that several Devonshire Regiment soldiers on airfield guard were killed in one German raid, and two airmen in another.

'In one low level attack by three Heinkel IIIs, the asbestos roof of the hangar which still stands to the left of the terminal building approaches was shattered and there are still cannon shell holes in some of its main girders,' says Ginger. 'Sixteen of our aircraft on the ground were damaged.

'The raiders usually came in from the south-east. If we had warning of just a couple of raiders we would scramble two fighters, if it looked like being a large raid we would scramble everything available.'

During a single German raid on the airfield in April 1941, the bombs pictured here all failed to explode and were defused by the bomb disposal unit. This picture was given to the airport archives by Douglas Ramsay, a New Zealander who served at the airfield with 504 (County of Nottingham) Squadron as fitter-armourer. He says the assortment of UXB's included 250lb, 500lb and 1000lb.
The men L to R are: W.O. Turner; Airman Stanton; Airman Parkes; Airman Ramsay.

'My pilot, Teddy Holmes, treasured as a souvenir a Luger pistol which had belonged to one of the German pilots he shot down.'

Sergeant-Pilot Haw of Ginger's squadron claimed the squadron's first Exeter combat engagement on 17 January 1942 when he damaged a lone Heinkel.

Pilots from 504 were billeted in what is now the Gipsy Hill Hotel at Pinhoe and the airmen used to spend their off-duty evenings in Exeter. Ginger met Hazel, the local girl who became his wife, at a dance in the old Civic Hall. He was one of many men from the airfield who married local girls. He returned to Exeter after the war and became an air-frame rigger on the Airport staff, originally with the Civil Anti-Aircraft Unit. Since retirement in 1965, he has worked for NCP as an airport car park attendant.

Another Exeter veteran who first came to the airfield during the war is Exeter Flying Club's Chief Flying Instructor, Wing Commander Ted King. He was posted to Exeter as a pilot with 131 Spitfire Squadron in 1943, returning after the war as a pilot with CAACU and became flying club CFI in 1972.

With fellow officers he was billeted at a county mansion, Farringdon House, a few miles from the airport, which was later to become a Home Office approved school for girls.

'It was a beautiful place with lovely grounds in which to relax when you weren't on duty,' recalls Ted.

'On duty our squadron flew in and out of Exeter on sorties until shortly after

CLOAK AND DAGGER

EXETER WAS ONE of the wartime airfields from which allied agents took off to be landed in enemy occupied France says veteran airport staff man Ginger Davies.

While with the RAF there in 1941, he twice saw impressive limousines arrive with blinds drawn to hide their occupants.

The car drove to a far edge of the airfield where one or more of the people in the car would go aboard a waiting Lysander aircraft. It was of the type used for transporting agents, and had a fixed outside ladder.

'We were kept well away from it,' says Ginger. 'Exeter would have been convenient for flying agents to the Cherbourg peninsula.'

Exeter Flying Club's Chief Flying Instructor, Wing Commander Ted King pictured in the cockpit of his Spitfire VII when he was flying from Exeter as a pilot with 131 (County of Kent) Squadron in 1943. He fell in love with Devon and returned after the war as a pilot with the CAACU.

D Day in 1944, or we flew from the associated fields at Bolt Head, Culmhead or Harrowbeer for which Exeter was the section station.

'We made regular fighter sweeps over France attacking trains, convoys and other military targets, and we would escort other formations attacking German shipping. On D Day we gave support to the invasion forces, mostly attacking behind the invasion beaches. Our losses were minimal and I can't ever remember not getting back into Exeter.'

Many of the airfield's wartime buildings are still in use for industrial and other purposes. Looking around the flying club building Ted King observes: 'When I was a Spitfire pilot here, this was the RAF blacksmith's shop.'

Mrs Mary Carnall who has lived in Clyst Honiton all her life says: 'I was a pupil at the village school when the airport was built on Mr Hawkins's Waterslade Farm. I used to go to the farm with his daughter Margaret who was at school with me. When the first air raid siren went the teacher took us all to the church tower for safety. At night we used to go and stay at Broadclyst and it was lucky we did, because one morning we came back to find that our farm cottage had been bombed.

'We used to have special passes moving about in the vicinity of the airport, so the guards would let us through.

'In my teens I used to go to RAF dances with other local girls in the main airport building. One of my boy-friends was a pilot who went out on a mission but sad to say never came back.

'The camp's NAAFI manageress used to lodge at our house, and we also used to have some of the Polish airmen as lodgers.

'Some of us from the village used also to be invited to go and see film shows in the camp cinema, a building which a local farmer has since the war been using as a milking parlour.

'In the later stages of the war, in the build-up to the D Day invasion, the

Americans were stationed on the airfield. Some of them when they were given new uniforms used to bring the trousers to my mother to alter for them.

'But in the fortnight before D Day we didn't see anybody. They were all confined to the airfield. We didn't know it at the time but the extra noise of aircraft on D Day was because of all the machines taking off towing gliders behind them.'

One of the most hazardous flying operations carried out from Exeter during the war was that of the pilots of the research flight '02' which moved in from Farnborough in September 1939. It was commanded by Squadron Leader C.R.J. Hawkins. The RAF was seeking ways of cutting through the cables to barrage balloons over German war targets to enable its bombers to go in low. One of the almost suicidal jobs of the men of '02' was to fly into balloon cables to test various types of cable cutting devices. The tests were mainly carried out on the cables of balloons flown over Pawlett Flats near Bridgwater. A test pilot called A.E. Clouston is thought to have been one of the men involved. Men of the unit earned several Air Force Crosses for their part in what was described as 'This highly dangerous sport'.

Pilots of 131 (County of Kent) Squadron pictured near the Clyst Honiton village end of the airfield with one of their Spitfires.

EXETER MYSTERY

MYSTERY STILL SURROUNDS one Exeter operation of Whitsun 1943, which is believed to have ended disastrously for many of the aircrews involved.

No mention is made in any records at the airport today. But Michael Payne, now of Salisbury, who spent a lot of time at the airfield as a wartime air cadet, says that Venturas of No 2 Group set off for a raid on Cherbourg escorted by vast numbers of Spitfires.

He adds: 'I was there when the survivors returned, having been mauled by FW 190s over the Channel. As a cadet I helped to refuel the Spitfires, but we were kept away from the bloody remains of 464 Squadron's Venturas.'

Ground crews of 317 Polish Squadron pictured with their Squadron Leader and one of the Squadron's Spitfires. The Squadron flew from Exeter in 1941 and 1942. Seventh from left in the front row is Joe Wasniowski who returned to live in Exeter after the war.

The many successes of pilots of 317 Polish Fighter Squadron which was posted to Exeter from Acklington in May 1941, are remembered by Mr Jozef Wasniowski who now lives in retirement at Exwick, Exeter.

His work as a fitter-mechanic maintaining the engines of the squadron's Hurricanes and later Spitfires brought him to Exeter with them. But Joe has sad memories of what he calls a black day for the squadron when the airfield for once failed to live up to its enviable reputation for good visibility.

'Twelve of our aircraft had been out on a patrol over the English Channel and were in an engagement with enemy aircraft,' he says. 'Fog came down as they were making their way back and they were going round and round trying to land, and some began running out of fuel. Only two came down without damage. Some of the pilots were forced to bale out, and we lost ten aircraft, some of which crashed in fields near the airfield. Our squadron leader was killed and three pilots were injured.'

The decimated squadron was, however, rebuilt and stayed in Exeter until April 1942 when it was moved to Northolt. On 19 August 1942 it was one of five Polish squadrons which sent up 224 flights in one day for the raid on Dieppe.

Joe Wasniowski's squadron and 302 Squadron were part of a day fighter wing. Also Exeter based was 307 Polish night fighter squadron using Defiants and later Beaufighters and Mosquitoes which bore the emblem of an owl perched on a horned moon. They had the aid of ground-controlled radar direction finding interception units based on Exminster marshes and at Wrafton.

Joe recalls that one Defiant shot down an enemy bomber which crashed into the sea near Exmouth. A Squadron Leader Skalski shot down seven raiders and Flt. Lt. Rutwski another two.

One of 317 Squadron's main jobs was Channel patrols escorting sea convoys.

The car that really was hit by a Hurricane. It happened probably in 1941 when an airfield contractor's car came into conflict with a Hurricane of 504 (County of Nottingham) Squadron flown, it is believed by Flying Officer Vic Barnes. From the sodden state of the grass it seems to have happened during a wet spell. Mrs Teresa Tutt of Exmouth whose late husband flew with 504 kindly loaned the photograph. She says that FO Barnes and the contractor both escaped injury, but the Hurricane obviously needed a new prop.

'My job was to keep our fighters flying,' he says. 'They had to be checked and signed for and standing in readiness before dawn. We often worked until late in the night to have them ready.'

Joe was a men's hairdresser in Cracow before his national service with the Polish Air Force in 1936. He cheated death time and again after his country was overrun by the Germans, and eventually reached Gibraltar to join a British convoy to Liverpool in 1940. He was posted to a British bomber squadron in Scotland before being switched to 317 Polish Squadron when it was formed.

Joe married an Exeter girl and after the war returned to the city working for the Harper Aircraft Company at the Airport making aircraft parts, but he later returned to hairdressing as partner in a city centre business.

During the enemy raids on Exeter one Polish pilot of 307 Squadron shot down two Junkers 88's in just ten minutes.

The last Defiant of 307 Polish Squadron, aircraft No. 1671, is today on display at the Battle of Britain Museum in Hendon.

Three Czechoslovakian fighter squadrons were also for a time at Exeter, their Wing Commander Mrazek winning the airfield's first DSO.

For the first nine months of the war a civilian air link had been maintained with the Channel Islands, but that ended on 13 June 1940 when BOAC Capt S.T.B. Cripps landed his Ensign airliner at Exeter bringing Jersey Airways staff evacuated from Jersey before the German occupation.

RAF Station Exeter was officially formed on 6 July 1940, when the Hurricane fighter squadrons 213 and 87 were based there. The first station commander was Wing Commander J.S. Dewar, DSO, DFC, who had commanded 87 Squadron, but who was reported missing, believed killed in action, while on a flight from Exeter to Tangmere on 12 September 1940.

The two squadrons were already 'blooded' having been involved in bitter air battles over France prior to and at the time of the evacuation from Dunkirk. 213 had lost several pilots killed or taken prisoner of war. Others came back to the UK with the evacuation fleet. They had shot down numerous enemy planes. Flt Lt Wight was credited with ten and other pilots also recorded notable 'kills'.

No. 87 Squadron had fought right through the campaign in France, suffering losses and scoring many victories until they were pulled out leaving behind all their kit and equipment, and the squadron records as well.

The men of 87 Squadron lightly protested that 213 had bagged all the 'best' parts of the Exeter station. In fact 213's officers were living at Exeter's grand Rougemont Hotel.

The two squadrons made a major contribution to Exeter's involvement in the Battle of Britain. They covered the largest sector on the South Coast, and escorted convoys at sea on the Plymouth, Bolthead, Start Point to Torquay route. They also helped to defend the Portland naval base against German attack. On 10 July 1940, Pilot Officer Jay of 87 Squadron claimed one enemy aircraft shot down, but Pilot Officer Cock was himself shot down and had to swim ashore.

On 11 July, 213 Squadron intercepted enemy aircraft approaching a convoy off Portland and claimed two probable shoot downs. Sub. Lt H.G.K. Bramah, on attachment from the Fleet Air Arm, chased a Dornier from Portland to Dartmouth, but was shot down by the Dornier's return fire. He ditched, but was soon picked up.

On 19 July, some of 87 brushed with a formation of Ju87s over Portland in which an enemy rear gunner was hit. On 24 July, an 87 section over Devon saw a Ju88 being chased by fighters of another squadron, and joined in. Flying Officer R.P. 'Roly' Beamont (later to achieve fame as a test pilot), as reports of the time put it, administered the *coup de grace* near Tiverton.

On 25 July, Flt Lt Rayner damaged an Me110 south of Portland. For a while a night flight from 87 was detached to Hullavington, Wilts.

A sad accident for 87 came in a dawn take-off from Exeter at the end of July 1940, when two of their Hurricanes collided. Pilot Officer Darwin, whose father first formed the squadron in 1917 and was instrumental in its reformation in 1937, received head injuries which put him out of the Battle of Britain.

87 Squadron later concentrated on night flying using their Hurricanes in the night defence of Bristol, Cardiff, Exeter and Plymouth. German bombers were overhead almost nightly, their targets including Merseyside and South Wales. Another distinguised Exeter Polish Pilot, Wing Commander Jan Michaelowski, was killed in 1943 in a landing accident while avoiding another aircraft.

In February, 1942 three Dornier 217s flew up the River Exe to bomb the airfield, reportedly as a diversion to cover the escape of German warships

Pleased to home in on Exeter Airport in 1943 were the members of this Lancaster bomber crew. The wireless operator was Noel Deeble who now lives in Exmouth. 'I had reason to be grateful for the existence of the airfield in 1943. On 12 July we went on a bombing mission to Turin in Italy. Because of bad weather we flew back across France to the Bay of Biscay, up past the Brest Peninsula. By this time we were running short of fuel and so, after a ten hour flight we made it to Exeter and landed at 8.00am on 13 May. After refuelling we returned to our base in Lincolnshire and went on to complete a tour of ops.'

Scharnhorst and *Gneisenau* through the Channel. One of the Dorniers crashed beside the A30 east of Rockbeare village, after being hit by ground defences.

During 1942 Bomber Command began diverting crippled Blenheims, Wellingtons and Whitleys to Exeter, often with wounded men on board who were swiftly moved to hospital. Later, Halifaxes and Lancasters were diverted.

Among VIP's who went to see Exeter as an example of a typical fighter station was the then Lt-General (later to be Viscount) Bernard Montgomery.

During the build-up to the D Day invasion of France in 1944, some of the RAF units pulled out of Exeter to make way for the United States Army Air Force's 50th Troop Carrier Wing; 440th Troop Carrier Group and Squadrons 95–98, with forty-five glider towing Dakotas.

Exeter became known as Station 463 of the USAAF. The Dakotas went into intensive glider towing training and on D Day towed their paratroops to invasion dropping zones on the Cherbourg peninsula. Three of the aircraft were lost in the operation.

After a bridgehead had been established by the allied invasion forces, the Dakotas ferried out supplies from Exeter and brought back wounded men, for transfer to hospital.

Meanwhile Mosquitoes from Exeter went on long range 'intruder' missions behind the enemy line in France, flying on to refuel in Algiers.

And with the advent of flying bombs over Kent and London, Exeter's day fighters moved to Kent where they amassed a score of kills. Joe Wasniowski proudly recalls that pilots from his squadron would pursue the flying bombs, and hit on a knack of tilting them off course over open country and sending them crashing down usually without any harm to life or property.

As the invading forces advanced on the Continent, the RAF squadrons from the Exeter sector moved to keep pace with them and a comparative 'hush' came over the sector. Exeter's role in the Second World War had for the most part been completed.

BURIED TREASURE?

ANOTHER MYSTERY FROM the Second World War is still unsolved at the airport today, and it remains a fascinating topic of conversation. The puzzling question is: 'Did the United States Army Air Force, when it left Exeter after the war, bury massive quantities of unwanted aircraft and motor vehicle parts, and perhaps even complete aircraft, just to get rid of them?'

Talk is that the Yanks bulldozed a crater in the centre of the grass triangle between the runways, and buried all the unwanted gear in it. And it is hinted that a similar 'graveyard' of smashed up aircraft may exist elsewhere on the airfield.

It seems though that nobody has put these rumours to the test. You could, after all, do a lot of expensive digging and come up with nothing more than earth and stones in the end!

To mark VE Day a formation of Oxfords, Spitfires and Vengeances flew over Ottery St Mary, Honiton and Axminster, recalls Michael Payne, who as an Exeter air cadet was a passenger in one of the planes.

ROLL OF HONOUR

DOZENS OF RAF squadrons were at various times stationed at Exeter Airport during the Second World War, or at the airfields of Harrowbeer, Church Stanton (Culmhead) and Bolt Head, which formed part of RAF Station Exeter.

Two army units were also involved on the ground: one from the Devonshire Regiment to provide guards, and the other from No. 700 Construction Unit, Royal Engineers, which made the airfield usable again following enemy attacks.

The following Roll of Honour includes those squadrons or units known to have flown from Exeter or its subsidiary stations:

Royal Aircraft Establishment '02' Department which included research into ways of cutting barrage baloon cables.

Gunnery Research Flight, armoured testing section, testing guns and turrets.

213 and 87 Squadrons, Hurricanes.

263 Squadron, Whirlwinds. 601 (City of London) Squadron, Hurricanes.

Polish night fighter squadron 307, Defiants, Beaufighters, Mosquitoes. Polish Squadrons 302, 316 and 317, Spitfires and Hurricanes.

504 (County of Nottingham) Squadron, Hurricanes.

64, 126, 611 Squadrons, Spitfires.

310, 312 and 313 Czechoslovakian Squadrons, Spitfires.

257 and 266 Squadrons, Typhoons.

21 Squadron, Venturas.

131 (County of Kent) Squadron, Spitfires.

306 Polish Squadron, 610 (City of Chester) Squadron, 616 Squadron and 308 Polish Squadron, Spitfires.

247 (China-British) Squadron, Hurricane IIc's.

Section of 116 Squadron, Lysanders.

536 Squadron, Turbinlite Havocs.

286 Squadron, Master III's, Airspeed Oxfords (anti-aircraft co-operation).

Section of 276 Squadron, Lysanders and Walruses.

50th Troop Carrier Wing, USAAF with Squadrons 95 to 98, Dakotas.

No 3 Glider Training School, RAF.

222 Squadron, Tempests, Meteors.

329 Squadron (Free French) Spitfires.

151 Squadron, Mosquitoes.

691 Squadron, Vengeances, Harvards, Oxfords, Martinet (anti-aircraft co-operation).

WARTIME ROMANCE

A FIVE-BARRED gate on the edge of the wartime Exeter airfield led to romance and forty-one years of happy marriage for one of the airmen stationed there.

Mr Alan Taylor of Sweetbrier Lane, Exeter, first came to the airfield as an airframe fitter with 87 Squadron when it was re-equipped in 1940 after the evacuation from Dunkirk. Alan was among the survivors who got back to Britain.

He recollects: 'We were quartered in some huts on the opposite side of the airfield near the main Honiton Road. Close by was a fateful five-barred gate over which a pal of mine and I were tempted by two cheeky females to a nibble of potato crisps one day.

'You notice I said "fateful." "tempted," and "nibble." Well I'm still married to that cheeky female forty-one years later. She still keeps me in one lump bless her.'

Alan's five-barred gate was on the country lane which led to Waterslade Farm before the airport was built. The one-time RAF quarters there are now the pavilion for Clyst Rovers FC whose ground abuts the airfield.

When 87 Squadron first arrived the ground crews slept under canvas, and Alan still laughs about the night when the lads had sunk a few pints at the Honiton Inn, and forgot to slack-off their tent guy lines, with the result that the tent collapsed on them during the night.

'I woke to a beautiful view of the stars,' he says, 'but I could hear some awful language coming from under the tent where arms and legs were thrashing about. By then I was rolling in the grass laughing my head off. I was pounced on and my nose rubbed in "something".

'I made good friends with the village blacksmith who was quite a character. I often went to watch shoeing in progress. He was also the landlord of the Honiton Inn. That was our initial beginning on cider. Wow! Some nights we were glad of our hands and knees on our way back up the lane.'

Alan was at the airfield during frequent raids by the Luftwaffe but says the attackers didn't have it all their own way. 'One of our armourers fitted four Browning machine guns on a ground stand, and blow us all if he didn't manage to shoot down a Jerry aircraft which tried a low flying job over the aerodrome!'

5

THE AIRLINES

AN ADVENTUROUS ERA of enterprise in civil aviation opened up for the airport after the war, with several new airlines being launched and new routes opening up. It brought success for some and disappointment for others, but one success story was that of Jersey Airlines who in 1952 resumed their schedules from the Channel Islands to Exeter which had been disrupted by the war.

In 1962 their traffic was taken over by British United (Channel Islands) Airways who also operated services to Paris, Dublin, Cork and Belfast. In 1966 they introduced additional services to Edinburgh, Glasgow, Manchester and Southampton, and to cope with the increased traffic the Airport expanded its apron area in front of the main terminal building.

Harry Richards, now senior air traffic controller, who joined the Airport staff in 1963 proudly remembers how as many as five British United Vickers

Jersey Airlines re-open their Exeter to Channel Islands services in 1952 after disruption by the war. Local journalists about to board the Rapide for an inaugural flight are Cyril Payne (*Express & Echo*); Geoffrey Wareham (*Western Morning News*), now BBC; Sid Brown (*Express & Echo photographer*) and Frank Muscroft (*Western Morning News photographer*).

Viscounts might be on the apron all at the same time. The turbo jets, he says had passenger appeal as 'real airliners', and BUA were switching to BAC 111's which would be even more of an attraction to passengers.

'We were beginning to expand, the Viscounts were really putting Exeter on the air map,' Harry observes. But then came a dispute between BUA crews and their management about pay, and overnight, in July 1968, the Viscount services ended.

'It was a day of tragedy for Exeter,' Harry comments.

One of the BUA pilots was Geoff Whittaker. His experience of flying in and out of Exeter paid off when in 1980 he was bringing in a holiday charter from Santander, Spain, which ran out of fuel over Ottery St Mary. He brought the aircraft and its passengers down safely in a forced landing in the Otter Valley, about the only place where an aircraft of that size might have crash landed safely.

In 1968 British Island Airways was formed by an amalgamation of Jersey Airline, Manx Airline and Morton Air Services operating between Exeter, Jersey, Guernsey, Southampton, Belfast and Dublin.

A new enterprise for Exeter in 1961 was that of British Westpoint Airlines founded at the airport by the brothers Frank, Don and Jack Mann of Torquay, with Don as Chief Pilot.

They mostly used DC3 Dakotas, but also Rapides and a Dove, after acquiring the Plymouth-based Mayflower Air Services. They operated to the Scillies,

7

10

11

9

Newquay, and Plymouth, with the Dakotas mostly being used on the Exeter service to London (Gatwick) and from there flying on for Air France to other destinations.

Exeter Airport's manager in that period, Wing Commander Jack Pearse recalls: 'I had the highest hopes for those services, but there weren't at that time enough people to make it the resounding success it deserved to be.'

Westpoint's operations closed down in 1966, after which South West Aviation, also based at Exeter, applied for similar route licences with the addition of Bristol, Glamorgan and Penzance.

A bold venture in 1978 was Air Westward launched by the then chairman of Westward Television, Peter Cadbury. Using Cessna Titan aircraft (with WTV included in their registrations) on an Exeter to London service, the line was forced to close its Exeter operation after only a year. It was taken over by British Island Airways under the name BIA/Air West. Twenty-seven Exeter based staff lost their jobs, though twelve moved over to BIA.

During 1980, BIA, Air Anglia, BIA/Air West and Air Wales amalgamated to form the present Air UK, providing scheduled flights from Exeter to Ireland, Channel Islands, France, Holland, Glasgow, London (Gatwick) and Southampton.

Other airlines which have been associated with Exeter are British Eagle, British Midland, Cambrian, Dan-Air, Morton Air Services and Manx Airlines.

In 1985 Jersey European Airways made Exeter their operating engineering

1. Westpoint Dakota, 1963.
2. Westpoint Rapide, 1964.
3. British United Dart Herald, 1964.
4. Derby Airways Canadair C4, 1963.
5. Westpoint Dakota being serviced, 1962.
6. British Eagle Viscount, 1964.
7. British United Viscount, late 1960s.
8. Cambrian Airways Viscount, 1964.
9. Mercury Airlines De Havilland Heron, 1964.
10. BIA-Airwest Titan (after merger), 1979.
11. Air Westward Cessna, 1978.

and administrative HQ, and have remained firmly established there. Using Shorts 360, 36-seat 'mini jumbos', and Embraer Bandeirantes, JEA operate to the Channel Islands, to Paris via Jersey from Exeter, and to Belfast and Dublin. They recently added two Fokker F27's to their fleet.

Air UK use F27's to Jersey and Guernsey. Also now operating through Exeter to London are Plymouth based Brymon Airways whose twice-daily flights are used both by businessmen and leisure travellers.

Fifty years on from the days of the Railway Air Services Rapides, the airport is handling increasing numbers of jetliner flights for tour operators to such destinations as Tenerife, Majorca, Malaga, Alicante, Ibiza, Portugal, Spain, Greece and Yugoslavia.

The Airport is also now running regular night mail flights taking first class Westcountry post to Merseyside and the West Midlands, and returning with mail for the South West.

Politicians don't always get things right, but Sir Kingsley Wood seems to have hit the nail on the head with that description of the airport back in 1938 as a sound investment for the future.

THE BRISTOW CONNECTION

FOR A BRIEF spell in the 1970s, Exeter Airport was the base for a helicopter training operation.

It was run by Bristow's on behalf of Westland Helicopters of Yeovil, as a training unit to serve Westland's customers.

Groups of pilots came to the unit to familiarize themselves with the handling of new Westland machines. Among the fliers were military pilots from overseas countries which had chosen to buy from Westland.

Bristow's set up an impressive unit in portable single storey structures on the far side of the airfield from the main terminal buildings.

Israel's Yom Kippur war with Egypt in 1973 echoed over the airport when there were protests against the training of Egyptian helicopter pilots at the Bristow unit, and one protester 'buzzed' the airport in a twin-engined light aircraft he had flown from London.

6

THE CAACU

OLD HANDS AT Exeter Airport still speak with awe about pilot Sammy Samuel's amazing feat of airmanship.

It happened on 25 January 1956, when Sammy was on a routine flight from the airport in the cockpit of a Vampire jet. With colleague Harry Ellis flying close by in another Vampire, he was providing interception training for defence units, and the two were flying at about 10000 feet over the sea south of Bridport, and climbing.

Then Sammy's engine blew up.

Now retired and living at Woodbury Salterton near Exeter, he recalls: 'A tongue of flame shot forward from the engine intakes and flashed back over me. The main engine carcase had shattered, and there was a flame like a giant blowlamp trailing about 30 yards behind.'

Pilots and ground staff of the Civilian Anti-Aircraft Co-operation Unit, (CAACU), pictured here soon after the unit was formed in March 1951. Centre front is the then Airport Manager, Wing Commander Parkhouse. The aircraft is a Beaufighter. Picture by Eric Thompson, standing on extreme right.

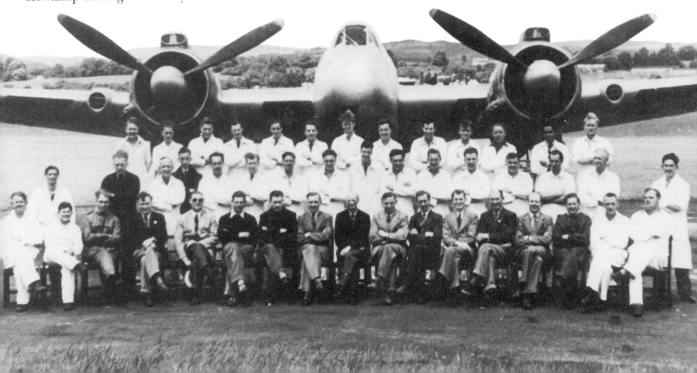

Pilot briefing before the last flight out of Exeter by CAACU Mosquitoes on 9 May 1963. Second from left is Sammy Samuel who won praise for gliding a Vampire jet 40 miles back to the airfield after its engine blew up. Third from left is Harry Ellis later to become Airport Manager.

Fortunately the fire didn't spread, and after sending out a May Day distress call, Sammy made his mind up to glide the unpowered Vampire something like forty miles back to Exeter.

With Harry Ellis holding a watching brief from the other Vampire, he made it. Emergency crews stood by at the Airport as Sammy was talked in by Air Traffic Control. The crippled Vampire came out of cloud over Farringdon House and Sammy brought it down to a perfect 'dead stick' landing beside the main runway. Virtually all it needed was a replacement engine.

Experts still praise the 40 mile glide as one of the finest feats of airmanship, and it earned Sammy a well merited green credit in his flying log.

Sammy was one of the many ex-RAF pilots who found jobs with the then operators of the airfield, Exeter Airport Ltd, in the Civilian Anti-Aircraft Co-operation Unit (CAACU) which the company operated under contract to the Ministry of Defence.

A break from Spitfire servicing for some of the CAACU ground staff, circa 1951–2.

The job of the unit, which ran from April, 1951 to December, 1971, was to provide training for the Army, Navy and RAF in combatting attack from the air. The CAACU aircraft tested radar defences, and some also towed drogues for target practice by anti-aircraft gunners.

At full strength the unit had twenty-six pilots, all ex-RAF, and in the twenty years of its history they logged a total of 75386 flying hours.

It was a sad day for the airport, and brought a marked reduction in flying activities when the CAACU job was switched in 1971 to service units, in particular No 7 Squadron, RAF at St Mawgan, Cornwall, using Canberras. Another fine piece of airmanship by a CAACU pilot was that of 'Bam' Beaumont. Taking off on a mission in a Vampire, he was carrying full drop tanks of extra fuel. As he was climbing away above the village of Clyst Honiton the Vampire suffered total engine failure.

Bam just had enough height to bank around towards Aylesbeare and release the drop tanks before completing his 'circuit' with a 'belly' landing on the grass of the airfield. And although injured, he lived to fly again.

Not all the CAACU pilots though, fared so well as Sammy and Bam. The unit had a commendable safety record but two pilots died in crashes. One tragically lost his life when the Spitfire he was manoeuvring over Bude, crashed. Another

Some of the CAACU aircraft pictured by Exeter enthusiast John Gregory
1. DH98 Mosquito, 1963
2. Gloster Meteor, 1965
3. Vampire in hangar, 1965

died equally tragically when his Vampire jet crashed while on approach for landing. He was making a tight turn into the main runway when he got into difficulties through a strong cross wind.

Target towing also brought its risks. On target towing over South Wales in a Meteor, Wing Commander 'Cass' Cassidy found that gunners on the ground shot at him instead of the drogue he was towing. A hole was shot through the tail of his Meteor, but he made it safe back to Exeter.

Roy Smallridge, now the airport's Senior Telecommunications Officer first arrived at Clyst Honiton as a 'temporary' recruit to the CAACU staff when it was formed in 1951. He remembers that the unit took up about half of the hangar now used by Westcountry Aircraft Servicing. The other half was still in use as a food store – a hangover from the war – and was full of eggs, butter and powdered milk, but within a matter of weeks all that had gone.

Roy recalls that the first pilot appointed for CAACU was Jack Trill who became chief pilot. Another of the pilots was Harry Ellis who was chief pilot for most of the life of the unit, also becoming eventually the airport's director.

He says that in the 1950s landing aids were primitive by comparison with today's equipment. They had to rely on an old direction finding apparatus and

transmitters and receivers. These had come to the UK during the war on lend-lease and were in fact very reliable.

The airport was also the base, from May 1949 to June 1954, of the RAF's No. 10 Reserve Flying School using Tiger Moths, Chipmunks, Ansons and Oxfords. Pilots would visit the airport for a week at a time to do their training.

Roy's records show that CAACU began in 1951 with Beaufighters, Spitfire Mk 16's and Oxfords.

The records run as follows:

Beaufighters, 1951–54; Spitfire Mark 16, 1951–52; Oxfords, 1951–57; Spitfire Mark 21, 1952–54; Mosquito 35's, 1953–63; Spitfire Mark 16, 1954–56; Vampire pure jet, 1954–59; Ansons, 1956; Balliols, 1957–58; Vampire T 11s, 1961–71; Hunter Mk 4–7, 1960; Meteors, 1962–70.

CAACU aircraft were also used in the making of two epic films: *Reach For The Sky*, the story of fighter ace Douglas Bader; and *633 Squadron*, the story of the raid on a heavy water plant in Norway.

CAACU used four Spitfires from RAF Henley for use in the Bader film. It

A bit of a prang on a rainy day for a Balliol of CAACU. Ground staff arrive to clear up.

One of Exeter's CAACU Spitfire's painted in false colours for its part in making *Reach For The Sky*. Kenneth More, who played the part of fighter ace Douglas Bader, is in the centre.

The men in white overalls are (left) Joe Andrews, engine fitter, and Jeff Morrish, rigger. With elbow in cockpit is pilot George Hickson, and with Kenneth More is pilot Pete Morgan (who loaned the picture). On the extreme right is pilot Alec Ince and standing on extreme left is John 'Snagger' Stokes, Telecommunications Officer.

also provided three pilots, Alec Ince, George Hickson and Pete Morgan, all of whom made good friends with the film's star, Kenneth More.

One of the Spitfire's used in the filming is now on show at Auckland War Museum in New Zealand, while a Mosquito used in *633 Squadron* is at the Hendon Museum.

Pete Morgan, now back in Exeter after years of civil flying in Zambia, recalls: 'In the making of *Reach For The Sky*, they had to use water paint to give our Spitfires the authentic squadron markings. But every time it rained the markings washed off. They had to keep someone standing by with a fresh can of paint to put the markings back!'

7

THE FLYING CLUBS

OVER THE FIFTY YEARS of Exeter Airport's history, hundreds of people have qualified as amateur pilots there, thanks to the Aero Club and its successor, Exeter Flying Club. And the flying lessons continue today.

The Aero Club was founded in 1937, almost a year before the airport originally opened. It was a commercially run club as distinct from the present day members' club.

It was founded and run by the Straight Corporation as part of their agreement to operate the airport on behalf of its owners Exeter City Council. Aviation pioneer Whitney Straight, then in his mid twenties, was its first chairman. As previously stated he had spent some of his boyhood at Dartington Hall in Devon and himself learned to fly with Mr W.R. ('Parky') Parkhouse at the Haldon airstrip.

About to take off for their honeymoon in an Aero Club Hornet on 1 October 1938, are club member Gordon Taylor and his bride Vera Newton. The Vicar of St Mark's, Exeter, Rev. J.H. Freeman, wishes them happy landings. Mr Taylor was one of the fifty-four club and Exeter Air Guard pilots who flew with the RAF or Navy in the Second World War.

Aero Club refuelling old style. An Auster by the pumps in 1963.

Piper Cub with old control tower in background, 1966. An American doctor flew the Cub across the Atlantic, landing on Exeter canal. The Cub then had floats fitted, but was back on its wheels for this picture.

The Exeter club's first quarters, including the bar, were at the back of the first hangar to be built on the airfield. When the terminal building was completed it provided comfortable quarters including lounge, dining room, squash court and sun terrace. The facilities were virtually identical to those of other Straight Corporation aero clubs in other parts of the country.

Within two years the club's membership had grown to three hundred plus 123 associated members of the Civil Air Guard unit which had been formed at the airport.

The first airport manager, who was also the Chief Flying Instructor, was Capt L.R. ('Jock') Mouatt, who was succeeded temporarily by Jack Pearse, and then by Flt Lt R.L. Bateman, and for a brief spell before the Second World War by 'Parky' Parkhouse.

The club's dining room was the setting for many a social occasion, and club member Gordon Taylor, now boss of Exeter paint firm W.E. Taylor and Son, held the reception there after his marriage in October 1938 to Miss Vera Newton, at St Mark's Church, Exeter. They took off for their honeymoon in one of the aero club's Hornet Moth biplanes.

When the war broke out, Mr Taylor was one of the fifty or so Aero Club members who became pilots in the RAF or (as in his case) the Fleet Air Arm. He still pilots his own helicopter.

The Aero Club closed down during the war, and was re-opened by Mr Parkhouse around 1949 after he had become the airport's first post-war manager.

Airport and Flying Club personalities at a conference for flying instructors in March 1980. The Airport Director, Harry Ellis, is on the extreme left, and his predecessor, Jack Pearse, on the extreme right. Fourth from left is the Chief Flying Instructor, Ted King.

In the mid sixties the club closed down, and the airport was without one until 1971 when the present-day Exeter Flying Club was formed by a nucleus of people who came from the nearby Dunkeswell Club.

Chief Flying Instructor, Wing Commander Ted King recalls: 'We started in a tiny office behind the radio hangar before moving into our present spacious building overlooking the airfield in 1972. This was one of the buildings erected for the RAF during the war, and when I was stationed here as a pilot with a Spitfire Squadron, it was the blacksmith's shop.

'When I returned after the war as a pilot with the Civilian Anti-Aircraft Co-operation Unit it was a drogue packing room.'

The club's first chairman in 1971 was Brian Claridge, boss of Westcountry Aircraft Servicing. He is now serving a second term of office. Chairmen in the interim were Keith Chambers, Ian Cummings and Dennis Kirkby.

The first Chief Flying Instructor in 1971 was Dickie Dougan, who was succeeded by Rufus Heald and then by Ted King.

The club house now includes a lounge and bar area, briefing rooms and offices. It is a thriving club with more than five hundred members and seven club aircraft, in addition to privately owned machines. The club planes are five training Cessna 150/152s and two Cessna 172s.

An Aero Club member of 1938 suddenly transported into today's club scene, would, though, be shocked at what club flying now costs. An "A" licence pilot's complete course in 1938 cost between £12–10 shillings and £20 according to the type of aircraft used, whereas to obtain the equivalent qualification today wouldn't leave much change out of £2500. Hire of a club aircraft in 1938 cost as little as £1 an hour, while it today costs in the region of £50.

8

SKILFUL TOUCHES

A Dakota of the RAE stands outside a wartime hangar, in use for servicing during the 1970s.

DAYS WHEN A revolutionary new type of light aircraft was built at Exeter Airport are remembered by Colin Pugh, the Airport's resident Civil Aviation Authority approved welder.

Colin, who has a wizard's den of a workshop in a former RAF wartime building a stone's throw from the main terminal, reflects that if only the design had caught on, Exeter might have become the base for a manufacturing operation to rival Cessna.

Sad to say it didn't. Only a small number of the single-engined high wing monoplanes were built by the Chrislea Aircraft Company which operated in the years just after the Second World War from a hangar type of factory just off the main airfield.

Colin recalls that two versions were built, the Chrislea Super Ace and the Chrislea Skyjeep. The latter was an air ambulance version with a hinged back through which casualties on stretchers could be loaded.

Colin's recollection is that it had an unconventional control system and that there may have been problems certifying it.

Exeter aircraft enthusiast John Gregory says that the Chrislea Ace prototype was designed and built by R.C. Christophorides at Heston, before production was switched to Exeter in 1946. The first one flew at Exeter in February 1948. Test pilots were Rex Stedman and D. Lowry. Colin Pugh remembers that another test pilot was Alfie Burroughs.

John Gregory recalls that the Chrislea machine replaced the conventional joystick and rudder bar with a single wheel mounted on a column which protruded from the dashboard on a universal coupling. A total of seventeen of the planes was produced. Work on another nine was started, but abandoned.

John believes that three of the Chrislea machines still survive. One, a Skyjeep, was recently restored and is flying at Bathurst, New South Wales, Australia. Another, a Super Ace went to Pakistan in 1950, was brought back to the UK in 1985 and is now flying from Bodmin. A third Chrislea, another Super Ace, is still in use somewhere in the North of England.

The Chrislea plant was taken over by Harper Aircraft Company which was itself succeeded by Exeter Aircraft Company. Colin Pugh joined that company in 1954 as an airframe fitter.

'In those days we were making parts under sub-contract to Vickers Armstrong for the Varsity, Viscount, Valiant and VC10,' he recalls. 'Then we came on the airfield itself to make test equipment for Rolls and parts for the Britten Norman Islander.'

Since Colin formed his own business at the airport, he has designed and built a working platform, the Bak Jak which has become internationally popular in the aircraft industry. It is a working platform which makes working in prone, or near prone positions much more comfortable.

The manufacturing activity in which he was involved for Exeter Aircraft Company was a peacetime continuation of skills developed during the war when Spitfires were assembled at Exeter in a link with the Exeter motor firm, Pike's of Alphington Street.

One of the Exeter built Chrislea Ace light aircraft pictured in August, 1949, by Michael Payne, now of Nunton, Salisbury. Photo courtesy of Mr Payne.

The Pike's workshops provided a local manufacturing facility for Spitfires. Exeter's new Plaza Leisure Centre now stands on the garage site. The old Chrislea factory is, now occupied by Spenco.

Though many support industries and manufacturers have come and gone, the skills needed in the service and repair of aircraft continue as an essential element in the life of Exeter's busy airport.

Westcountry Aircraft Servicing, headed by Exeter Flying Club Chairman Brian Claridge has earned a world-wide reputation for its skills in restoring vintage aeroplanes, Dakotas in particular.

Early in 1988 the company was completing in its giant hangar a major overhaul of the last four-engined Lancaster bomber. The bomber belongs to the RAF's Battle of Britain Memorial Flight. Westcountry's main task, though, is that of looking after the wide variety of other aircraft in general use today.

Another major servicing facility is that provided by Jersey European Airways who have established the maintenance base for their fleet at Exeter.

All of this activity is good for Exeter's economy. The Airport in 1988 is providing employment for something like four hundred people, including the Jersey European and Westcountry operations. The terminal operators, Airports UK, have a staff of about seventy.

The Airport also stands ready to fight oil pollution whenever a spillage occurs in the seas around the coast of the Westcountry. It's the base for one of the country's anti-pollution flights which uses aircraft fitted with tanks full of a special detergent to counter any oil spills and disperse them safely. Low-level spraying of a dispersant from the air has been found a fast and effective way of tackling the spills.

PROGRESS

Roy Smallridge, Senior
Telecommunications Officer, has
been with the airport since 1951.

EXETER AIRPORT HAS phased out the little man with the tinny voice. He has been replaced by an altogether smarter character called ILS, and the change has been welcomed by the many airline captains who come in to land there says the airport's Senior Air Traffic Control Officer, Harry Richards.

Harry, who first joined the airport staff in 1963 after RAF service, admits he was once among the ranks of the little men with the tinny voices himself. It's his way of referring to the old talk-down approach system on which air traffic control had to rely before today's Racal Decca ILS (Instrument Landing System) was installed as part of a £3 million Devon County Council improvement programme to bring the airport out of a proud past into a promising future.

The massive programme took four years and was completed in 1981. It included an extension of the main runway by 230 metres to 2081 metres, upgrading of the terminal building and the installation of omni-directional runway lighting and precision visual slope indicators as well as the ILS system.

As Harry Richards proudly observes: 'We are now about the leader in the country for the type of equipment we have acquired.' The improvement programme indeed fitted Exeter for its role as regional airport of the South West and equipped it for virtually any demands presented by air traffic development for the foreseeable future.

But it wasn't always like that. Harry remembers: 'When I arrived in 1963 there were no instrument approach aids. We had a cathode ray direction finder which gave bearings on each aircraft's radio transmission. Using the bearings we could give a controlled descent through clouds until the pilot was able to make his own visual final approach.

'Then in 1965 we took a major step forward when we updated the equipment with Decca 424 radar and a non-directional beacon, plus our first permanent electric lighting for the runway. This meant we could do surveillance radar approaches. The pilot followed instructions from ground control, allowing an approach down to 360 feet on the main runway 26, or to 270 feet on the 08 runway from the opposite direction.

'But the airliner captain of today no longer wants to hear a little man with a tinny voice giving him instructions. He wants to lock-on to an instrument landing system and interpret his own approach. Airlines throughout the world now expect that and we can provide it.'

The airport also brought itself up to international standards when it cut the distance between runway lights from 100 yards to 60 metres.

In 1984 it led the rest of the country when it updated its radar to take it into the next century. It bought the Plessey Watchman system virtually off the drawing board. And says Exeter's Senior Telecommunications Officer Roy Smallridge: 'It seems we made the right choice. The system has since been bought by the RAF, and the Civil Aviation Authority is going to use it to replace the old systems at all the state operated airports. We now have landing aid equipment as good as any major airport in the country.'

The Watchman enables Exeter's air traffic controllers to keep watch on all aircraft movements through their area, and thus to prevent any threat of 'conflictions'.

Roy has worked at the airport since 1951 when he joined the Civilian Anti-Aircraft Co-operation Unit, and he recalls the only runway lighting they had in those days was provided by goose necked flares, placed on either side, and by

The old and the new. The oblong tower photographed in 1963 reveals something of its wartime vintage, while Harry Richards stands in the new aircraft control tower which is equipped with every modern navigational aid.

One of the bigger modern jets now using Exeter. The Paramount Airlines DC9 was on the apron in 1987.

two giant mobile landing floodlights whose power came from a generator driven by an engine. They were towed by tractor into position at the end of the runway.

At the terminal building itself, that £3 million scheme completed in 1981 included a new control tower with 360 degree visibility, extended passenger lounges, bar, restaurant, buffet, new public viewing verandah, new airline sales and inquiry offices and improved luggage handling facilities. There was also a new conference room for forty people, and a VIP lounge, both with catering facilities.

The improved terminal was officially opened on 13 July 1981, by the Chairman of the British Tourist Authority, Sir Henry Marking. It has given sterling service to an increasing number of passengers ever since, the 166 268 going through the terminal in 1987 being a forty per cent rise on the previous year. In 1987 some 325 719 kg of freight was handled.

And the current talk is of the possibility that Exeter might in the future begin handling direct flights from the USA for the first time.